SURRENDER:

Surrendering It All To Gain It All

SURRENDER:

Surrendering It All To Gain It All

ROSZIEN KAY LEWIS

CONFESSIONS
PUBLISHING

Surrender: Surrendering It All To Gain It All
Copyright © 2020 Roszien Kay Lewis
ISBN: 978-1-7359-6200-9

Printed and bound in the United States of America.

Editor: Erick Markley

CONFESSIONS
PUBLISHING

Confessions Publishing is a subsidiary of Roszien Kay LLC, Lancaster, CA 93536

For information regarding discounts on bulk purchase and all other inquiries, please contact the author directly at roszien@gmail.com

AUTHOR'S OTHER BOOKS

Confessions of An Overcomer: From Tragedy to Triumph

Confessions of An Overcomer: The Truth About the Wait

Getting Spiritually Snatched

Submit, Resist, Flee: Strategies to Living a Victorious Life

Hidden Preparation

The Wilderness

CONTENTS

FOREWORD

I consider myself to be an extremely blessed individual who witnessed parents operate in two of the fivefold gifts (Evangelist, Prophet) our Lord and Savior gave to edify the church. And now, I can not express the joy I feel to observe my niece, Evangelist and Prophet Roszien operate under the same Spirit who influenced my mother and father to encourage and instruct the body of believers they served. I stand in awe as I hear the prophetic voice of God provide clear instructions to those he loves through this anointed vessel.

If you have faith to believe that today is the rise of the prophetic, then you should rejoice that God has chosen to reveal his plan to his people through prophet Roszien. Just as king Johoshaphat said in 2 Chronicles 20:20(b), "Hear me, O Judah and you inhabitants of Jerusalem: Believe in the LORD your

God, and you shall be established; believe His prophets, and you shall prosper." I hear that same voice of the Lord calling and instructing those with a sincere heart and a burning desire to stand in the secret place of the Lord God Almighty to hear and obey what prophet Roszien is saying to you if you want to prosper. Listen people of God to what the LORD is saying. Then He said, "Hear now My Words; If there is a prophet among you, I, the LORD, make Myself known to him in a vision; I speak to him in a dream." Prophet Roszien, continue to be relevant in this dark hour that we may have hope for the future. Continue to allow God to speak to you as we hear his voice through you. The sign of a true prophet is that their words come to pass. Prophet what is God saying about the condition of the world today?

Elder Jerome Chism

PREFACE

PREFACE

❧

Surrenderance: though many claim to surrender, it is an area many believers are falling short in. The reasons for this falling short vary from person to person. One person may have an issue surrendering completely to God because of their distrust. Another person's inability to completely surrender to God may be because of ignorance. While others' inability to fully surrender to God may be because of complete rebellion. While yet another person's inability to surrender may be because they really don't know what's required of them.

The sad reality is that there are way too many opinions, doctrines, and theories in the land that have caused much confusion about what is required. The truth is this: God's Word lays out the requirement for surrenderance. According to Matthew 16:24-25 (KJV), "*Then said Jesus unto his disciples, 'If any man will come after me, let him deny himself, and take up his cross, and follow Me...'*" Based on these passages of scripture, surrenderance to Jesus requires us to:

1. Come after Him,
2. Deny Ourselves,
3. Take up Our Cross,
4. and Follow Him.

As straightforward as it seems, surrenderance is still something that many continue to struggle with. Because of this, I found it necessary to follow the leading of the Holy Spirit and write this book. In the preceding pages you'll learn what Jesus meant in Matthew 16:24-25.

THE DRAW

CHAPTER I:
THE DRAW

—————————— ∿ ——————————

When one first reads Matthew 16:24, the assumption is made that *we* decide to "come after" Jesus. In support of this assumption, many point to the fact that God has given us freewill to make choices for ourselves. Although this assumption seems correct, it isn't completely correct.

In order for anyone to "come after" Jesus, one must first be drawn by God. According to John 6:44, Jesus declared, "no one can come to Me unless the Father who sent Me draws him and I will raise him up at the last day." The Greek word for "draw" is *helkuo,* which means to "drag" literally or figuratively. In essence, the drawing of one to Christ is one-sided. We have absolutely nothing to do with it. We merely exercise our freewill by responding to God's drawing after He has initiated it.

The way in which we are drawn to God varies. One can be drawn through a sermon they heard. Others can be drawn by a dream or vision. While others can be drawn the way I was drawn: by a knock. I literally woke up one day at the age of 26 years old and said, "I think I need to go to church." At that time, I had a live-in boyfriend, was actively engaged in fornication, as well as other sins, and had not attended church in a long time. I believed God was real because my grandparents were actively involved in church and took every opportunity to talk to us about God. I had actually felt his spirit on the rare occasions I went to church as a young child. I even would pray and ask Him not to allow me to die in my sins.

Up until the time of this drawing I had no desire to get to know God. To be honest, after that initial thought about going to church, I still didn't move. It literally took days before I acted upon it. During that time between Him drawing me and me actually making the first step of going to church, He kept on knocking. I literally was faced with Revelations 3:20. God kept on knocking on my heart until I decided to open the door and let him in by going to church to hear about Him.

There was no way I made this decision on my own. At that time, I loved the life I had been living. I was living my dream. I was in law school, had moved to a new state, was madly in love and in a relationship with an amazing man, had amazing friends, and was financially stable. I thought I had everything I needed.

In my mind, I didn't need God because life appeared to be good. Little did I know, I needed a Savior. And I was incapable of understanding this. Therefore, God had to be the one to initiate contact with me.

The reason why God had to initiate the drawing for me, as well as for everyone else that comes to Jesus, is because we are all incapable of coming to Him on our own. The natural man (aka our flesh) has absolutely no desire or ability to come to God. In our natural state, the heart is hard, and our minds are darkened. We don't have a desire for God or the things of God. Our only desire is to fulfill the desires of our flesh.

Now, I know some of you may be a little confused by my previous statement. Honestly, I was initially confused by this biblical truth. I thought I was the one who decided to surrender to God. I did not consider the fact that I was only able to make the choice to "come", after God had initiated contact with me. In hindsight, I now realize He had been working on me for years.

I can recall feeling His presence at a very young age. Around 5 or 6 to be exact. I would literally sit in church as praise and worship was being offered up to Him by the adults, engulfed in heat. I wanted to dance. I wanted to shout. I wanted to run. But I did nothing as I sat there with my heart almost pounding out of my chest.

For some odd reason, I was scared. Scared because I didn't understand what was wrong with me. Even though nothing was really "wrong" with me, at that time I had no idea that the presence of heat was a sign that the Holy Spirit was present. I had no idea that God had allowed my elementary school self to experience His presence so strongly.

Feeling God's presence wasn't the only means He used to draw me to Jesus. God used His holy vessels as well: my grandparents and a friend I had met in college. My grandparents had become key vessels throughout my life because they would plant "gospel" seeds into everyone who came into their home. They did this by talking to us, young and old alike, about God and His word.

With every conversation, there had been an impression left on the surface of my heart and mind. So much so that I would daydream about what was said to me for weeks at a time. These conversations ultimately continued until they both passed away.

These conversations had been so important to me then, I craved them as an adult. I would literally drive from San Diego California to their home in Los Angeles CA to hear them speak about God with so much passion, love, and kindness. I did this the most when I felt unloved, overwhelmed with life stressors, and when I experienced hopelessness. During those instances, I had no idea how instrumental and important those conversations were.

When I went off to college, God placed a friend in my path who truly lived for Him. There we were 18 years old, in college, and able to do whatever we wanted. But she decided to continue to live for God every single day! Christina was literally a living epistle placed in my path to continue planting seeds on behalf of God.

She literally invited Him into every conversation. I recall crying and venting to her about issues I had with my then boyfriend. Instead of encouraging me to leave him or do to him what he had done to me, she encouraged me by talking about God and my future God given husband.

It didn't stop there, she invited me to church with her. We would literally church hop on occasion instead of partying. I really enjoyed this time with her. Over a short period of time, I started to admire her a lot because of her love and dedication to God.

She had the relationship with Him that I desired to have. She had the strength I did not have. The strength to say yes to God and no to her flesh.

Christina continued to be used by God to plant seeds into me until I stopped spending as much time with her. There had been no disagreements either. I just changed. My life changed. My time changed. I became engulfed in school, work, partying, and dating. I was navigating through my own issues and process in life.

During that time, I would go years without stepping foot into church. I no longer went with her, and I rarely went to visit my grandparents. But when I did go to visit them, they continued planting as if there had been no interruption.

Fortunately for me, God had a plan that would reunite Christina and I. At the age of 25, I had been applying to different law schools in CA. To my surprise, I had either gotten denied or wait-listed. I was devastated and worried. Fear hovered over me. For the first time in my life it seemed as if I would be forced into a place where my educational career would be over!

My back was against the wall. I truly believed my plan of going to law school was not going to happen. I recall picking up the phone and having a conversation with Christina. At that time, she was in a PHD program at Michigan State University. During that conversation she encouraged me to apply to Thomas M. Cooley Law School. Prior to that conversation, I hadn't considered applying to a school out of state. However, after we talked, I put all my faith into that basket and immediately applied. To my surprise, I received an acceptance letter immediately after I had settled on plan B, becoming a probation officer.

Upon receiving the acceptance letter, I knew God had done it. I accepted the fact that I was meant to pick up and move from San Diego CA to Lansing Michigan. I knew it was a part of God's plan for my life. I was sure of it because I had prayed—yes, you read correctly. The person who hadn't really prayed or went to church, placed her future in God's hand.

At that time, neither one of us knew what providential move had taken place. Christina thought she was helping a friend pursue her dreams of going to law school. I thought that I was merely embarking on another journey of fulfilling one of my lifelong dreams—nothing more, nothing less. Little did we know that this move was a part of God's plan for my life. Little did we know that this move would put me in the right place, at the right time, in the right state of mind for God to come knocking on my heart Himself.

In hindsight, had God not done all that He had done, I wouldn't have come to Him on my own. God had to be the one to initiate me coming to Him. I enjoyed the life I had been living. My mind did not know or could not comprehend that there was more for me. I thought I had an amazing life.

Furthermore, I could not discern what God had been doing around me because I was carnal. According to 1 Corinthians 2:14 (KJV), "But the natural man receiveth not the things of the Spirit of God: for they are foolishness unto him: neither can he know them, because they are spiritually discerned." When God sent my grandparents to plant seeds, I couldn't discern that it was God because of my carnal mind. When I was going from church to church with Christina, I could not hear or feel God pulling me. No matter how He used them, I wouldn't change.

Although He sent them to be the bridge between Him and I, I wouldn't cross over. I wouldn't decide to go to God on my own behalf without begging for Him to rescue me out of my foolishness. Instead, I used those He had sent me to lead me. I used their relationships and connection with Him for my benefit. I used their revelation of who He was to make me feel better in those moments when my life wasn't going so well. I literally would get my fix of Jesus from them each time I needed it.

This cycle I had continued all the way up until God came knocking on the door of my heart. It all continued until He initiated the draw. And surprisingly to me, I came! It wasn't until the moment that I decided to respond to God knocking on my heart that I became an active participant. It wasn't until that moment that my God given freewill came into play.

Prior to the moment that God started knocking on the door of my heart, my freewill had not been a factor at all. Why? As stated previously, because of my carnal mind—which is a mind that is not subject to the law of God, one which refuses to take orders from the Holy Spirit—I lacked the desire and ability to "come after" Him. However, when the knock occurred, the veil of ignorance had been removed.

FREEWILL

Mankind was given freewill by God when He originally created Adam and Eve in His image and likeness. Therefore, mankind was created with the innate ability to choose. Initially this ability was amazing. However, things quickly turned from amazing to horrible as a result of Adam and Eve's disobedience.

God instructed Adam and Even to not eat anything from the tree of the knowledge of good and evil. To make a long story short, as a result of one conversation between Eve and the serpent, they decided to disobey God. As a result of their disobedience, their eyes were opened to good and evil.

As a result of the act of two people, their nature, as well as the nature of mankind, was changed. No longer did they enjoy the benefits of being in a sinless state (Genesis 1:27). Literally, the image of purity and godliness that they once had, was over. And what's even worse is that now this new wicked state was imputed to their children in all mankind. According to Genesis 5:3, Adams' image and likeness, not that of God, was passed along to his son Seth. But even before the birth of Seth, sin nature had manifested itself in Cain when he murdered his brother Abel as a result of his envy (Genesis 4:8). Literally from generation to generation, sin nature was passed down.

Now, our sin nature, also known as the "flesh" stands in direct opposition to God. In fact, there is a constant war being waged by our flesh against God.

For the sinful nature is always hostile to God. It never did obey God's laws, and it never will. 8 That's why those who are still under the control of their sinful nature can never please God."
(Romans 8:7,8)

"But people who aren't spiritual can't receive these truths from God's Spirit. It all sounds foolish to them and they can't understand it."
(1 Corinthians 2:14)

"The sinful nature wants to do evil, which is just the opposite of what the Spirit wants. And the Spirit gives us desires that are the opposite of what the sinful nature desires. These two forces are constantly fighting each other, so you are not free to carry out your good intentions."
(Galatians 2:14)

"What is causing the quarrels and fights among you? Don't they come from the evil desires at war within you?"
(James 4:1)

"Dear friends, I warn you as temporary residents and foreigners to keep away from worldly desires that wage war against your very souls."
(1 Peter 2:11)

After reading this, I know that a part of you may disagree. Or for those who haven't really surrendered to God, or for those who have partially surrendered to God, you may be thinking, "but I'm a good person. I do good to people; this cannot be true." To be honest, I thought the same thing until I completely surrendered to God. To get a clear understanding of what is really going on, we must look at "The Doctrine of Total Depravity."

THE DOCTRINE OF TOTAL DEPRAVITY

This doctrine states that in every aspect, man is flawed. The good that we do, that which is inside of each and every one of us in our natural state (i.e. those good deeds we do as a good person), is only the remnant of God's image that we were formed with. But even this remnant of good is corrupted. Therefore, it is safe to state that within every person there is a mixture of good and evil.

Coincidentally, even our good intentions and good deeds may arise and come from mixed motives when we are without God. Sadly, the good in us cannot always be trusted. I'll say that another way, the good deeds that we do out of the "kindness" of our hearts when we are not fully surrendered to God, cannot be trusted. Why? Because they, as a result of our carnal state, aren't completely pure. There are times that we act out of deceit as a result of us being conniving, or out of our own interests and selfish motives. As difficult of a pill as it is to swallow, it's true.

Furthermore, according to the Doctrine of Total Depravity, sin nature is universal in humanity. We all have a sinful nature which affects every aspect of our lives, including our hearts. Consider the following scriptures:

"The human heart is the most deceitful of all things, and desperately wicked. Who really knows how bad it is?"
(Jeremiah 17:9)

"And I know that nothing good lives in me, that is, in my sinful nature. I want to do what is right, but I can't."
(Romans 7:18)

"But the things that come out of a person's mouth come from the heart, and these defile them. 19 For out of the heart come evil thoughts, murder, adultery, sexual immorality, theft, false testimony, slander. 20 These are what defile a person."
(Matthew 15:18-20 NIV)

"All of us, like sheep have strayed away. We have left God's path to follow our own. Yet the LORD laid on him the sins of us all.
(Isaiah 53:6)

"So the trouble is not with the law, for it is spiritual and good. The trouble is with me, for I am all too human, a slave to sin."
(Romans 7:14)

"Not a single person on earth is always good and never sins."
(Ecclesiastes 7:20)

"If we claim we have no sin, we are only fooling ourselves and not living in the truth."
(1 John 1:8)

"For I was born a sinner. Yes, from the moment my mother conceived."
(Psalm 51:5)

Because of our state of depravity, we cannot come to God unless He initiates us through the convicting of the Holy Spirit. He literally awakens in us a previously unknown interest in spiritual things. He also creates in us a new desire for these spiritual things. As this spiritual awakening takes place, the ability to use our free will to choose God kicks in.

As stated previously, as God started knocking on my heart, a desire for Him was ignited. This desire for Him led me to go to the only place I knew I could find Him: in the church. Once I used my free will to go to church, I started to thirst and hunger after the spiritual things more than ever before. This thirst and hunger subsequently led to me no longer craving various carnal things.

Literally in an instant, my ears were opened. My heart now became inclined towards God. His word began to actually mean something more than mere words written on a paper and placed in a book. They now became more than rules. They became life to me.

I began to have a desire for God that engulfed my entire being. This occurred because my heart changed. I now had this burning desire to know Him; to obey Him; to love Him. And to walk in all that He had promised.

This all occurred because of God. He had drawn me. After being drawn, I decided to use my freewill to choose Him. Ultimately, I chose to receive the free gift of salvation.

SALVATION

One cannot truly come after God without first receiving the free gift of salvation. The biblical definition of salvation refers to the deliverance from the consequences of sin and involves the removal of sin. In essence, it is the deliverance from God's judgment of sin.

> *"And since we have been made right in God's sight by the blood of Christ, he will certainly save us from God's condemnation."*
> *(Romans 5:9)*

> *"For God chose to save us through our Lord Jesus Christ, not to pour out his anger on us."*
> *(1 Thessalonians 5:9)*

Remember, it was sin that separated us from God. According to Romans 6:23, "For the wages of sin is death, but the free gift of God is eternal life through Christ Jesus our Lord."

When I used my freewill to go to church, it literally put me exactly where I needed to be to receive salvation. I literally heard the gospel of Jesus Christ—the good news of Jesus' death and resurrection. After hearing, I then believed in my awakened heart (Romans 1:16). After believing in my heart, I confessed with my mouth according to Romans 10:9-11: *"If you openly declare that Jesus is Lord and believe in your heart that God raised him from the dead, you will be saved. 10 For it is by believing in your heart that you are made right with God, and it is by openly declaring your faith that you are saved. 11For 'Everyone who calls on the name of the LORD will be saved.'"*

UNDENIABLE TRUTHS ABOUT SALVATION

1. **Only God can remove sin and deliver us from sin's penalty.**

> *"For God saved us and called us to live a holy life. He did this, not because we deserved it, but because that was his plan from before the beginning of time—to show us his grace through Christ Jesus.*
> *(2 Timothy 1:9)*

"He saved us, not because of the righteous things we had done, but because of his mercy. He washed away our sins, giving us a new birth and new life through the Holy Spirit.
(Titus 3:5)

2. God saved us through His son Jesus Christ.

God sent his Son into the world not to judge the world, but to save the world through him."
(John 3:17)

3. Jesus' death on the cross and subsequent resurrection achieved our salvation.

"For since our friendship with God was restored by the death of his Son while we were still enemies, we will certainly be saved through the life of his Son."
(Romans 5:10)

"He is so rich in kindness and grace that he purchased our freedom with the blood of his Son and forgave our sins."
(Ephesians 1:7)

4. Salvation is the gracious, underserved gift of God.

> *"...that even though we were dead because of our sins he*
> *gave us life when he raised Christ from the dead. (It is*
> *only by God's grace that you have been saved!)*
> *(Ephesians 2:5)*

> *"God saved you by his grace when you believed. And you*
> *can't take credit for this; it is a gift from God."*
> *(Ephesians 2:8)*

5. Salvation is only available through faith in Jesus Christ

> *"There is salvation in no one else! God has given no other*
> *name under heaven by which we must be saved."*
> *(Acts 4:12)*

> *"For this is how God loved the world: He gave his one*
> *and only Son, so that everyone who believes in him will*
> *not perish but have eternal life."*
> *(John 3:16)*

> *"For God has not destined us for wrath, but to obtain salvation*
> *through our LORD Jesus Christ."*
> *(1 Thessalonians 5:9)*

THE BOTTOMLINE: Where coming after Jesus is concerned, an undeniable truth is that we can only come after God has drawn us to Him. Then, and only then, are we able to come to Him and receive the free gift of salvation.

THE DENIAL

CHAPTER II:
THE DENIAL

Many people flock to altars around the world to receive salvation. For those who aren't flocking to the altars of a church, they receive the salvation of the Lord in their homes, cars, or whatever place they decide to call on Him. Unfortunately, some stop there. You read correctly: some people won't move further than receiving the salvation of the Lord.

For those who continue on their journey after receiving salvation, they too may stop short of experiencing the full benefit of salvation and being in a relationship with Jesus Christ. This stoppage is the reason why some, although they have received salvation, live defeated lives.

You may be wondering, why go through the process of receiving salvation if you aren't going to go all the way. Well, that's a good thing to wonder about. The answer is this, many stop at salvation because of cost. Now, if you think back to the scriptures mentioned in the previous chapter, you may recall that salvation is free to us. We don't have to pay a price for it. Jesus Christ paid the price because we were incapable of doing it due to our sinful nature.

Although this is an undeniable truth, there is still something that we must do after receiving salvation. We must live like Christ lived! Apostle Paul urged the church in Corinth "*...give your bodies to God because of all he has done for you. Let them be a living and holy sacrifice—the kind he will find acceptable. This is truly the way to worship him*" (Romans 12: 1).

An essential part of being a true follower of Jesus Christ is to live a life of self-denial. Self-denial involves the renouncing of oneself as the center of existence and recognizing Jesus Christ as one's new and true center. It requires us to be willing to deny ourselves of things such as possessions, status, dreams, and desires in order for us to grow in holiness and commitment to God.

"I once thought these things were valuable, but now I consider them worthless because of what Christ has done. 8 Yes, everything else is worthless when compared with the infinite value of knowing Christ Jesus my Lord. For his sake I have discarded

everything else, counting it all as garbage, so that I could gain Christ."
(Philippians 3:7,8)

When we deny ourselves, we acknowledge that the fleshy *self* (that part of us that is naturally inclined to fulfill human will) is dead. By doing this, we also acknowledge our new life is now hidden in Christ Jesus.

"For you died to this life, and your real life is hidden with Christ in God. 4 And when Christ, who is your life, is revealed to the whole world, you will share in all his glory. 5 So put to death the sinful, earthly things lurking within you. Have nothing to do with sexual immorality, impurity, lust, and evil desires. Don't be greedy, for a greedy person is an idolater, worshiping the things of this world."
(Colossians 3:3)

When we deny ourselves, we overcome the persistent fleshly demand of our body. The more we deny our carnal self (our flesh) and bring it into submission to God's word, the more we are less likely to give into sin. The bottom line is this: self-denial leads to us crucifying our flesh and living a life that is holy and acceptable to God.

"Those who belong to Christ Jesus have nailed the passions and desires of their sinful nature to his cross and crucified them there."
(Galatians 5:24)

Submit yourselves therefore to God. Resist the devil, and he will flee from you."
(James 4:7 ESV)

SELF-DENIAL MUST BECOME DAILY

The act of denying ourselves cannot be done just once, it must be done daily. Self-denial must be done for the rest of our lives here on earth. Why? Because when we surrender to God, our flesh still remains unsubmitted to Him. Our flesh now becomes at odds with our spirit man (the part of us that has surrendered to God).

The harsh reality is this, denying oneself isn't an easy task by any means. It can only be done through the power given to us by the Holy Spirit. I believe the struggle which is experienced between our flesh and spirit is explained perfectly by the Apostle Paul in Romans 7:15-25:

"15 I don't really understand myself, for I want to do what is right, but I don't do it. Instead, I do what I hate. 16 But I know that what I am doing is wrong, this shows that I agree that the law is good. 17 So I am not the one doing wrong; it is sin living in me that does it. 18 And I know that nothing good lives in me, that is, in my sinful nature. I want to do what is right, but I can't. 19 I want to do what is good, but I don't. I don't want to do what is wrong, but I do it anyway. 20 But if I do what I don't want to do, I am not really the one doing wrong; it is sin living in me that does it.

21 I have discovered this principle of life—that when I want to do what is right, I inevitably do what is wrong. 22 I love God's law with all my heart. 23 But there is another power within me that is at war with my mind. This power makes me a slave to the sin that is still within me. 24 Oh, what a miserable person I am! Who will free me from this life that is dominated by sin and death? 25 Thank God! The answer is in Jesus Christ our Lord. So you see how it is: In my mind I really want to obey God's law, but because of my sinful nature I am a slave to sin."

I don't know about you, but every time I read the above passages of scripture it becomes more and more apparent to me that it is only by God's grace and the power of the Holy Spirit that we learn to deny ourselves.

"11 For the grace of God has been revealed bringing salvation to all people. 12 And we are instructed to turn from godless living and sinful pleasures. We should live in this evil world with wisdom, righteousness, and devotion to God, 13 while we look forward with hope to that wonderful day when the glory of our great God and Savior, Jesus Christ, will be revealed."
(Titus 2:11-13)

As we practice self-denial, we grow in Christ. This is because as our flesh is being crucified with consistent practice, our spirit man (the part surrendered to God) grows stronger and develops more. All while the flesh is being weakened. The more our flesh is weakened, the more we are willing to submit to God. The more we submit to God, the more we become Christlike.

THE BOTTOMLINE: When coming after God, you cannot neglect to deny yourself! This denial includes all of your natural motives and impulses that conflict with God's Word.

TIPS ON HOW TO DENY YOUR FLESH

1. WATCH AND PRAY

> *"Keep watch and pray, so that you will not give into temptation. For the spirit is willing, but the body is weak!"*
> *(Matthew 26:41)*

It's imperative that every believer live a lifestyle of prayer. Prayer is simply communicating with God. In prayer, we speak followed by us listening for a response from God. I must be honest: God does not immediately respond all the time. When this occurs, you must not get discouraged. Instead, continue to pray and leave room for Him to speak.

You must live a lifestyle of prayer for a few important reasons. In prayer is where God will oftentimes reveal to us the traps of the enemy. In prayer is where God may decide to reveal to us areas that we need to straighten up in. Or even areas where we are vulnerable.

2. READ GOD'S WORD REGULARLY

> *"For the word of God is living and active, sharper than any two-edged sword, piercing to the decision of soul*

and/or spirit, of joint and of marrow, and discerning
the thoughts and intentions of the heart."
(Hebrews 4:12)

The more you read God's word the more you'll learn about Him. The more you learn about Him, the more you learn about what is pleasing to Him. The more you learn about what is and isn't pleasing to Him, the more you'll understand what is expected of you. The more you know what's expected of you, the more you'll be able to deny your flesh.

3. PRACTICE OBEDIENCE/SUBMISSION

"But the Helper, the Holy Spirit, whom the Father will
send in My name, He will teach you all things, and
bring to your remembrance all things that I said to you."
(John 14:26)

Because our natural inclination is to do what pleases our flesh, we must be willing to abort that inclination when it goes against what we know is desired by God. Now, I know that some of you may be thinking, "how do I know what's desired by God." Well, you've read above about reading and learning His word. Now, when it comes to actually obeying it, that's where the Holy Spirit comes into play. For those who aren't familiar with Him, the Holy Spirit is Jesus' Spirit and God's Spirit that dwells within those who ask for Him. You read right: you must ask for Him. The Holy Spirit is a gift from God that is available to all believers.

The Holy Spirit is the one that helps believers to obey and submit to God. The Holy Spirit is the one who knows the mind of God (1 Corinthian 2:16). The Holy Spirit leads and guides believers. The Holy Spirit gives us the power to say no to our flesh.

To overcome our flesh, we must practice obeying and submitting to the direction of the Holy Spirit. By doing this on a regular basis, we become stronger and stronger over time.

4. FASTING

> *"Howbeit this kind goeth not out but by prayer and fasting."*
> *(Matthew 17:12 KJV)*

There will be times that it will be difficult for you to deny yourself. This occurs because some habits are easier to let go of than others. In situations where you know that you cannot deny your flesh and obey God, it's important that you incorporate fasting to break the stronghold, addiction, or desire.

Fasting is starving your flesh through denial. Most often denial of food is done. However, some believers also will deny themselves of other things (i.e. social media). During the time of fasting, it's extremely important that you read the Bible and pray to God.

5. SUBMIT AND RESIST

Submit yourselves therefore to God. Resist the devil, and he will flee from you."
(James 4:7 KJV)

One way to triumph over the flesh is to submit to God and resist the devil. As stated before, the flesh wants to do what's pleasing to it. Oftentimes, that which is pleasing to it is sinful. We know that the devil is the one that's behind sin. Therefore, the more you practice submitting to God, the more equipped we will be to resist the devil. The more we resist him, the more we defeat him. When he's defeated, he'll leave us. But don't become relaxed because he WILL come back again.

6. TAKE THE WAY OF ESCAPE

"The temptations in your life are no different from what others experience. And God is faithful. He will not allow the temptations to be more than you can stand. When you are tempted, he will show you a way out so that you can endure."
(1 Corinthians 10:13)

When you find yourself in a situation where you are faced with fulfilling the desires of your flesh that are against God, and in danger of turning away, take the way of escape provided. Before you start thinking that there isn't a way of escape, let me stop you there. There is always a way of escape. We tend to ignore it. Next time, instead of ignoring the way out, take it! I promise that you won't regret it.

7. PLACE YOUR MIND ON THE THINGS OF GOD

"Think about the things of heaven, not things of earth."
(Colossians 3:2)

When we are working on denying our flesh, we must deny ourselves certain thoughts too. Mainly because ". . . *each person is tempted when he is lured and enticed by his own desire. Then desire when it has conceived gives birth to sin, and sin when it is fully grown brings forth death.* (James 1:14-15 ESV)." Our thoughts, if not sinful in themselves, can lead us into sin if we aren't careful. Consider this: ". . . *everyone who looks at a woman with lustful intent has already committed adultery with her in his heart"* (Matthew 5:28 ESV).

The way in which we place our minds on the things of God is by changing the way we think. We literally have to go through a process of renewing our mind. According to Romans 12:2 (ESV), *"Do not be conformed to this world, but be transformed by the renewal of your mind, that by testing you may discern what is the will of God, what is good and acceptable and perfect."* To renew our minds, we have to reject that which is acceptable by the world but violates the Word of God. We must put on the mind of Christ—a mind that is obedient to God no matter what.

To do this you must shut down thoughts which aren't in agreement with God's Word. You have to cast aside things like anxiety, fear, lust, as well as other thoughts. Instead you must ". . . *fix your thoughts on what is true, and honorable, and right, and pure, and lovely, and admirable. Think about things that are excellent and worthy of praise.* " (Philippians 4:8).

What you focus on will determine your outcome!

THE CROSS

CHAPTER III:
THE CROSS

THE MISCONCEPTION OF THE CROSS

Believers incorrectly assume that taking up their cross has to do with the issues of life. Some people interpret "cross" as some burden that they must carry in their lives. Burdens like strained relationships, a job where they aren't appreciated, or even physical illness. I have heard many say "this is the cross I have to bear" when they're suffering persecution. I've even heard it when someone is experiencing trials and tribulations. Or when they are experiencing a wilderness or pruning season.

Although these occurrences in life are real, they aren't what was on Jesus' mind when He talked about taking up our cross. In fact, those things mentioned above aren't even just a part of the life of a believer. If you'd be honest, you'd admit that these things are normal life occurrences in both the believer and unbeliever's life.

Let's be clear, as Jesus carried His cross up Golgotha, He wasn't thinking about the cross as being a burden He had to carry. Jesus was thinking about the painful death He would experience for the sins of the world!

HISTORICAL SIGNIFICANCE OF THE CROSS

To a person who lived in the first century, the cross meant one thing and one thing only: death by the most painful and humiliating means a human being could endure. The cross was symbolic of not just any death either; death by the cross was the most disgraceful form of execution. It was brutal torture. Torture which was reserved for slaves, foreigners, revolutionaries, and vile criminals.

The torture experienced by the cross carrier didn't start when they were placed on the cross. It started long before that point: it began with flogging. Flogging involved those convicted being repeatedly hit with a whip (which was made up of several pieces of leather and bone) or a rod inside of the city. Followed by them carrying the top part of their cross, which weighed between 75-125lbs, to the crucifixion area outside of the city walls.

As if this wasn't enough, they were put to greater shame and humiliation by having their crimes publicly broadcasted. Their charged offense was written on something for everyone to see and was carried by one of the Roman soldiers that occupied them to the crucifixion site.

At this time, they weren't thinking about simply carrying a burden in life. Instead, they thought about the pain they were experiencing as a result of the open wounds on their back. They were thinking about the heavy weight of the cross upon their weakened body. They were thinking about the death that they were soon to face once they reached the crucifixion site.

THE TRUTH ABOUT THE MULTITUDES AND THE CROSS

The multitudes who followed Jesus were vast. They would travel with Him from city to city. They did this to witness Him performing miracles, signs, and wonders. They did this to listen to Him teach.

Those who accompanied Jesus came from different backgrounds. Some were those He had healed. Some accompanied Him because they needed healing and deliverance. While others were mere onlookers.

Those who followed Jesus were those who were convinced, by no fault of Jesus, that He was going to free them from the oppressive Roman rule. They believed that He would do this by bringing a glorious kingdom to earth. Unfortunately, not only did the multitude of people possess this erroneous belief, Jesus' disciples did as well.

"And as they heard these things, he added and spake a parable, because he was nigh to Jerusalem, and because they thought that the kingdom of God should immediately appear."
(Luke 19:11 KJV)

You may be wondering, "how in the world did they arrive at this erroneous thought." Well, they arrived there because of their misunderstanding concerning the prophecies about Jesus' coming.

As a result of their flawed thinking, when Jesus started to talk about death to self and taking up their cross, they were utterly shocked. They had no desire to die, neither were they prepared to. Because there was great dislike for Jesus' teaching, the multitude started to leave Him by droves.

THE ENTIRE TRUTH ABOUT TAKING UP THE CROSS TODAY

Today, like during Jesus' time, many believers have a misunderstanding about being a disciple of the Lord Jesus Christ. Honestly, I was one of them, I thought giving my life to Christ meant my life would become perfect. I incorrectly assumed I'd be able to still follow my own path and reap blessings on top of blessings because I now belonged to the Lord. I just knew that health, wealth, and prosperity were all now my portion.

I had no idea taking up my cross and carrying it meant death, and at times, humiliation. Once I came to this realization, I had a choice to make: I could leave like the drove who followed Jesus, or I could take up my cross and carry it as I relied on the help of the Holy Spirit.

Taking up our cross as Jesus requires is costly. It requires commitment to Jesus to the point that we are willing to give up our hopes, dreams, and desires. Taking up our cross and following Jesus means that we are willing to die in order to follow Jesus.

If you're wondering whether you've taken up your cross, or whether you are willing to take up your cross, ask yourself the following questions:

1. Am I willing to follow Jesus if it means losing some of my closest friends?
2. Am I willing to follow Jesus if it means loss of my reputation because of false accusations (remember this happened to Jesus. It's what got Him to the cross)?
3. Am I willing to follow Jesus if it means losing my job?
4. Am I willing to follow Jesus if it means losing my life?

As hard as it is to answer those questions, you must not only consider them, but you must answer them. And after you do so, you may have to shift your mindset. Why? Because taking up your cross and following Jesus is non-negotiable! Don't believe me, consider the following passages of scripture:

"And he that taketh not his cross, and followeth after me, is not worthy of me."
(Matthew 10:38 KJV)

"For whosoever will save his life shall lose it: but whosoever will lose his life for my sake, the same shall save it. 25 For what is a

man advantaged, if he gain the whole world, and lose himself,
or be cast away?"
(Luke 9:24,25 KJV)

I know this seems harsh, but it isn't. It's a condition of being a disciple of Christ. Jesus made this crystal clear in Luke 14:27 when *He* said, *"And if you do not carry your own cross and follow me, you cannot be my disciple."* As a disciple, we are required to take up our cross daily even though it causes suffering to our flesh.

Before you decide to abandon being a disciple of Christ, I need you to understand something. We should be willing to endure for Christ because He endured for us. As a believer, we should be willing to "die to self" because Jesus died on the cross so that we could live! Nothing in this life is worth keeping if it means losing eternal life.

THE BOTTOMLINE: Taking up our cross is a call to absolute surrenderance, no matter the cost or pain. Although this can be tough at times, the eternal reward is definitely well worth the temporary pain.

THE FOLLOW

CHAPTER IV.
THE FOLLOW

~

To follow means *"to obey instructions or to do something according to a plan or someone's advice."* To follow Jesus means that we follow the example that HE has left behind. This means that we will no longer follow our friends, popular culture, family, or our selfish desires. Instead, we set our eyes on Him and Him alone. We place His instructions, desires, and plans for our lives above our own. We literally give Him complete control over our lives. And we do this through the leading of the Holy Spirit.

Remember, the Holy Spirit is God's Spirit and Jesus' Spirit that dwells within believers that accept Him. He is a free gift to believers given by God to assist us as we walk through life. The Holy Spirit is our Advocate. The Holy Spirit is our teacher. The Holy Spirit is our Guide. The Holy Spirit is our comforter. And He is the truth.

"And I will ask the Father, and he will give you another
Advocate, who will never leave you."
(John 14:16)

"But the Comforter, which is the Holy Ghost, whom the Father
will send in my name, he shall teach you all things, and bring
all things to your remembrance, whatsoever I have said unto
you."
(John 14:26)

"But I will send you the Advocate—the Spirit of truth. He will
come to you from the Father and will testify all about me."
(John 15:26)

"When the Spirit of truth comes, he will guide you into all
truth. HE will not speak on his own but will tell you what he has
heard. He will tell you about the future."
(John 16:13)

Now, you may be wondering why you would need the Holy
Spirit when following Jesus. The truth is the Holy Spirit is
needed because we cannot follow Jesus in our own strength—
no matter how good our intentions may be. Before you start
formulating arguments to refute this claim, let's take a look at
His disciples. They walked with Jesus for three years learning,

observing, and participating in Him performing miracles. They literally had a front row seat at times. They could literally see Him and reach out and touch Him. Although this was the case, they still could not follow Him faithfully in their own strength.

"'The Spirit alone gives eternal life. Human effort accomplishes nothing. And the very words I have spoken to you are spirit and life. 64 But some of you do not believe me.' (For Jesus knew from the beginning which ones didn't believe, and he knew who would betray him."
(John 6:63,64)

THE TRUTH ABOUT FOLLOWING JESUS

As mentioned above, God gave us the Holy Spirit because He knew that we would need a guide to help us. He also knew that it was inevitable that there would be times that we would struggle with obedience. God was well aware that even the strongest believer would have moments when they would really struggle with obeying Him and fulfilling His desires over obeying the flesh and fulfilling its desires.

God had also been aware of the fact that suffering was inevitable as we follow Jesus. I know that it seems odd that I would make this suggestion, but it really isn't. Part of following Jesus is enduring suffering at times. If I could be totally honest with you, suffering is common when following Jesus. Not convinced? Take a look at the scriptures below.

"If we suffer, we shall also reign with him. . ."
(2 Timothy 2:12 KJV)

"Yes, and everyone who wants to live a godly life in Christ Jesus will suffer persecution."
(2 Timothy 3:12)

As we follow Jesus, there will be moments when we find ourselves suffering persecution. Now, before we allow your mind to think about the extreme cases of being beheaded, consider the following definition of persecution first. According to the vocabulary.com definition of persecution, it means: *"unfair or abusive treatment toward a person or group of people,"* or *"hassling or singling out of a person or group because of race, religion. . ."* Although this is the case, be of good cheer because it will all work in your favor ultimately.

"And we know that God causes everything to work together for the good of those who love God and are called according to his purpose for them."
(Romans 8:28)

Aside from experiencing persecution as a result of following Jesus, you will face other difficulties. There will be times in your life where you will have to choose between following Jesus or enjoying the many comforts of life. There will be times when following Him will mean that you totally dedicate everything to Christ. You may face situations in which you will have to choose either Jesus or a relationship. You may have to choose between pleasing and being near your family or moving away to a place where God leads you. You may have to give up some hopes and dreams to follow Jesus as well.

Before you start panicking, let me make this really clear, Jesus isn't going to always ask us to do the hard things. But we must be willing to do them if asked! Jesus wants us to adopt a mindset that says: *"everything I have in my possession, I'll hold with an open hand. With a willingness to release it at any given moment if it is His will."*

THE GAIN

CHAPTER V:
THE GAIN

There are so many things you will gain by following Jesus. In fact, what's gained from following Jesus will always outweigh what is given up. For those who willingly give up things to follow Jesus, there are great rewards given to them on earth and in heaven. According to Mark 10:29-30:

". . . Jesus replied, 'and I assure you that everyone who has given up houses or brothers or sisters or mothers or father or children or property, for my sake and for the Good news, will receive now in return a hundred times as many houses, brothers, sisters, mothers, children, and property—along with persecution. And in the world to come that person will have eternal life.'"

Because this promise was made in the above passages of scripture, we can stand on it because God is ALWAYS true to His word!

"God is not a man, so he does not lie. He is not human, so he does not change his mind. Has he ever spoken and failed to act? Has he ever promised and not carried it through?"
(Numbers 23:19)

"It is the same with my word. I send it out, and it always produces fruit. It will accomplish all I want it to, and it will prosper everywhere I send it."
(Isaiah 55:11)

"For all of God's promises have been fulfilled in Christ with a resounding "Yes!' and through Christ, our "Amen" (which means "Yes") ascends to God for his glory."
(2 Corinthians 1:20)

Speaking of what God has promised, His promises are endless. And they are given as soon as you surrender and follow Jesus! Don't believe me? Take a look at some of the promises gained below.

1. God's Conditional Love

"For I am convinced that neither death nor life, neither angels nor demons, neither the present nor the future, nor any powers, neither height nor depth, not anything

else in all creation, will be able to separate us from the
love of God that is in Jesus Christ our Lord."
(Romans 8:38, 39)

2. You Are Never Alone

"Be strong and courageous. Do not fear or be in dread of
them, for it is the LORD your God who goes with you.
HE will not leave you or forsake you."
(Deuteronomy 31:6 ESV)

3. As You Draw Close to Him, He'll Draw Close to you

"Draw near to God and He will draw near to you."
(James 4:8 NKJV)

4. You Are Redeemed

"In him we have redemption through his blood, the
forgiveness of our trespasses, according to the riches of
his grace."
(Ephesians 1:7 ESV)

5. You Are Now Seated in Heavenly Places

"For he raised us from the dead along with Christ and seated us with him in the heavenly realms because we are united with Christ Jesus."
(Ephesians 2:6)

6. You Have a New Identity

"Therefore, if anyone is in Christ, he is a new creation. The old has passed away; behold, the new has come."
2 Corinthians 5:17 (ESV)

7. God's Plans for Your Life is to Prosper you, Not to Harm You

"For I know the plans I have for you," declares the LORD, "plans to prosper you and not to harm you, plans to give you hope and a future."
(Jeremiah 29:11 NIV)

8. All Things Will Work Together for Your Good

"And we know that all things work together for good to them that love God, to them who are called according to his purpose."
(Romans 8:28 KJV)

9. You Receive Strength to Do All Things

"I can do all things through Christ who strengthens me."
(Philippians 4:13 KJV)

10. You'll be Given Peace

"You will keep him in perfect peace, whose mind is
stayed on You, because he trusts in You."
(Isaiah 26:3 NKJV)

11. You'll be Given Power

"Behold, I give unto you power to tread on serpents and
scorpions, and over all the power of the enemy: and
nothing shall by any means hurt you."
(Luke 10:19 KJV)

12. You'll Be Given the Power to Overcome Temptation

"No temptation has overtaken you except such as is
common to man; but God is faithful, who will not allow
you to be tempted beyond what you are able, but with the
temptation will also make the way of escape, that you
may be able to bear it."
(1 Corinthians 10:13 NKJV)

13. The Devil will Flee from You

"Therefore submit to God. Resist the devil and he will flee from you."
(James 4:7)

14. The Weapons Formed Against You Won't Work

"No weapon formed against you shall prosper, And every tongue which rises against you in judgment, You shall condemn. This is the heritage of the servants of the LORD, And their righteousness is from Me," Says the LORD.
(Isaiah 54:17 NKJV)

15. You are Protected

"He shall cover you with His feathers, and under His wings you shall take refuge; His truth shall be your shield and buckler. You shall not be afraid of the terror by night, nor the arrow that flies by day, nor of the pestilence that walks in darkness, nor of the destruction that lays waste at noonday."
(Psalm 91:4-6 NKJV)

16. God Will Walk with You

"Though I walk in the midst of trouble, You will revive me; you will stretch out Your hand against the wrath of my enemies, and Your right hand will save me."
(Psalm 138:7 NKJV)

17. You Will be Delivered from Your Fears

"I sought the Lord, and He heard me, and delivered me from all my fears."
(Psalm 34:4 NKJV)

18. You Can Ask Him for What You Want

"But if you remain in me and my words remain in you, you may ask for anything you want, and it will be granted."
(John 15:7)

19. You Have a Crown of Righteousness Waiting for You

"I have fought the good fight, I have finished the race, I have kept the faith. Finally, there is laid up for me the

crown of righteousness, *which the Lord, the righteous Judge, will give to me on that Day, and not to me only but also to all who have loved His appearing."*
(2 Timothy 4:7, 8)

20. You'll Have Everlasting Life

"For God so loved the world that He gave His only begotten Son, that whoever believes in Him should not perish but have everlasting life."
(John 3:16)

21. Your Suffering Will Bring Great Glory

*"For our light affliction, which is but for a moments, is working for us **a far more exceeding and eternal weight of glory**, while we do not look at the things which are seen, but at the things which are not seen. For the things which are seen are temporary, but the things which are not seen are eternal."*
(2 Corinthians 4:17, 18)

22. You Will Be Conformed to the Image of Christ

"For who He foreknew, He also predestined to be **conformed to the image of His Son, that He might be the firstborn among many brethren."**
(Romans 8:29)

23. Jesus Will Come Again for You

"In My Father's house are many mansions; if it were not so, I would have told you. I go to prepare a place for you. And if I go and prepare a place for you, **I will come again and receive you to Myself; that where I am, there you may be also."**
(John 14:2-3)

24. God Will End Suffering

"And God will wipe away every tear from their eyes; there shall be no more death, nor sorrow, nor crying. There shall be no more pain, for the former things have passed away."
Revelation 21:4 NKJV

THE BOTTOMLINE IS THIS: when you completely surrender IT ALL to God and follow Jesus, you'll always gain more than you'll ever give up! Because of this, the surrender will always be well worth it!

CONCLUSION

CONCLUSION

God knew that we would experience difficulties as we journeyed down the road to absolute surrenderance. Despite this, He was so gracious to allow Jesus to not only be an example for us, but to leave us with instructions that would stand the test of time. But not only that, He was gracious enough to allow Jesus to come back and dwell within us!

Because of this, we are left without excuse. Rather, we are left with everything we need to not only come after Jesus, but what is needed to deny ourselves, pick up our cross, and follow behind Jesus for the rest of our lives.

Let's continue to surrender it all, to gain it all . . .

ABOUT THE AUTHOR

Roszien Kay Lewis is an emerging leader and catalyst with a prophetic voice. She has a deep rooted desire to see people healed, delivered, and set free. As a result she founded Destined to Be Released Ministries, a ministry whose sole objective is to encourage, teach, and equip others through the Word of God. Roszien has hosted conferences, workshops, and spearheaded the " 21 Day Jump Start My Draw" prayer challenge.

As a result of the trauma she suffered in her childhood and teenage years, Roszien formed #ConfessionsOfAnOvercomer motivational speaking company. Through this company she shares her testimony of overcoming every obstacle in her life. And she encourages others that they too can overcome anything as long as they believe in themselves.

When Roszien is not ministering to or mentoring others she's busy assisting others with book publishing. She is the sole owner of Confessions Publishing, a Christian based publishing company that assists authors with "turning their manuscripts into a masterpiece."

Roszien resides in California with her two beautiful daughters, Aaliyah and Myah.

CONTACT ROSZIEN

FACEBOOK: ROSZIEN KAY LEWIS

IG: ROSZIEN KAY LEWIS

EMAIL: roszien@gmail.com

www.ingramcontent.com/pod-product-compliance
Lightning Source LLC
Chambersburg PA
CBHW032118280326
41933CB00009B/900